Pouring Thoughts and Emotions into Poetry

AF624792

Kittay Kat

BookLeaf Publishing

Pouring Thoughts and Emotions into Poetry

Presentation by *BookLeaf Publishing*

Web: www.bookleafpub.com

E-mail: info@bookleafpub.com

ISBN: 9789357440592

First edition 2023

I dedicate this book to my parents, especially my mother. Thank you for all of your praise, guidance, and encouragement throughout the years. Without the both of you, I wouldn't be here and neither would this book.

I'd also like to dedicate this book to anyone who has ever felt lost in life- I've been there, too- in the dark chambers of my mind- but, have faith and trust that life gets better with effort and time. The future holds more brightness than you may be able to see right now; but, one day, that light will penetrate through and I hope you are able to view this book as a tool to help you get closer to the source of light that moves within you. It's already in there- just waiting to be found- so it can shine externally in it's own unique and beautiful way.

ACKNOWLEDGEMENT

Thank you to EVERYONE who has ever instilled any sort of hope and confidence in me to continue on my writing journey. I appreciate each and every one of you, as well as all of the continuous support and encouragement to pursue writing poetry!!

This ranges from teachers, to mentors, to counselors, family, acquaintances, and friends.

I want to give a special thank you to my hometown's library because I found my local writer's group through them in 2021, and also, for the countless years I spent perusing the bookshelves in search of stories to become engulfed in and, almost always, leaving with a nice pile of books stacked within my arms.

My current writer's group was not the first time I've gotten involved in a poetry/writing group, but it was the first time I had put myself out there in years and it was like having a fresh start in the right environment for me to begin growing. Thank you for the endless inspiration, motivation, and all of the support.

I would especially like to thank all of the friends I've encountered and met through livestreaming who have sat and listened to me read my poems aloud until I could barely speak, the poems that were emotional for me to read, the tears that spilled down my cheeks, the way they boosted my confidence and helped raise my self-esteem, the way they pushed me to go after my dreams.

Most importantly,
THANK YOU FOR MAKING ME FEEL SEEN!!!

Releasing Doubts Around Love

It appears to me, sometimes, that I view people
As if they're a shiny object
And I'm drawn to the new, bright light,
But, I know that's not quite right.
There's comfort there-
In finding someone who seems like me.
With passing time, however,
I see they aren't of my kind and
We really aren't so similar.
I know from previous relationships that not
everyone has the same heart as you-
And, although I want that,
I don't keep my hopes too high,
As I know from experience that the landing
Probably won't be dry.

Scared- that if I don't put myself out there in
some sort of an effort or attempt to try,
That new opportunities won't arise,
If, instead of going out, I simply sat inside.
But, I'm growing tired of getting dressed up,
only to go for a ride because I wasn't able to find
a cool place for me to hang out and vibe.

The bar isn't the right scene for a former alcoholic, nightclubs give me anxiety, and, the only option left;
The one that makes the most sense,
Feels like poetry meets-
However, the venues I'd like to check out are limited to certain days and times of the week that all seem to coincide with each other, on different sides of the state- which makes it hard to get from one place to another.
I'm stuck standing still-
Which is probably for my protection.
I know, right now, I'm supposed to be more focused on my life's direction.
But, I already know where I'm going..
I only long for a companion to join me for the ride.

The love I'm able to give
Isn't the kind that will shrivel up and die.
It's everlasting;
Which is why I want to make sure it's given to the right person,
Yet, it feels like they're nowhere in sight.
So, I'll journey through the nights,
In wander of my heart's desires
And release doubt and fear to the universe; to our higher power-

Having trust and faith that true love will,
Eventually, be acquired.

Free to Be Me

This room is like lightning,
And I'm floating on transcendent clouds.
Not bound by limiting beliefs
Because, right here, I can allow myself to be free.
Shaping my words into the form of poetry.
Even if I might be shaking with anxiety,
I know the feeling will fade eventually.
I can't allow fear to hold me back from the places I'm meant to go and see.
Each day brings new opportunities
For me to pursue and new goals to reach.

I feel like I've been climbing this ladder forever,
So, eventually, I have to reach the top sooner or later.
Getting to the top doesn't mean I won't still experience struggle-
I'll just be able to balance a little better
On stable ground;
Without having to cling to the bars
Or fearing losing my grip and falling all the way back down.
I know that I'll make it
Which is why I continue.

Even if my grasp slips
And I fall down a few rungs,
A little perseverance and determination help me climb back up.

Struggle is inevitable and it comes with levels-
Testing your endurance and flexibility.
You have resistance-
The ability to push back and fight for your right to continue to climb.
Don't let go of those bars,
Because you've already come too far to go back now-
And, if you let go,
You'll miss out on the wondrous opportunities life can bring forth
By letting go, you'll never get to see them or know.

By hanging on,
Even if you're dangling from one of the rungs,
You're putting faith, hope, and trust
That all will work out.
And in due time, it will.
Stay strong and show the world why you were put here.
Stand tall and secure in your talents and powers without the frightening feeling of fear.
Those talents are part of the key

To why you are here.
Hone them,
Own them,
Stop claiming that you don't have a talent or Not believing you're good enough at something you excel in.
Appreciate the gifts life has given
And align them to fit into your life's mission.

I Go Wherever I Feel Drawn

I go wherever
My soul feels called.
Sometimes that looks like me driving in circles,
Or venturing for hours.
Occasionally, I like to take my rest.
But, it's not usually long until I wake;
And then I'm off again
With purposeful intent
Or to wander in aimless directions.
It's hard for me to get lost.
I know so many areas.
But, once in a while, I travel far in search of new sights to experience.
I'm in love with the beauty of life,
The feeling that I have a sense of freedom.
In these moments, I am.
Free.

I Survive

I embody the energy of a warrior soul.
Even when I've tried to give up;
My body wouldn't allow me to cecede.

The hardships I've overcome
Speak of my strength
The nuisances I've been dealt with,
Have been learning lessons for my development.

Every waking day,
I survive
With each breath I take,
I'm beyond grateful that I've managed to make it this far.

Every step,
Shows perseverance;
Courage.
Courage I didn't realize I had before.
I wasn't able to see this clearly;
I used to be consumed with anxiety-
Riddled with worry,
Until I uncovered
The truth of my reality.

I was, previously, unaware of the fact that I have
adhd and what that actually meant for me.
I didn't discover this until I was 26.
26 years..
Thinking I must be crazy or that something was
really wrong with me.
The pieces just didn't quite fit.
Incorrectly diagnosed;
I was put on med after med.
I felt like a little guinea pig,
With most exacerbating my symptoms
Because they weren't the proper ones that were
needed
To help my head.

I begged and pleaded
For God, the universe, for anyone
To help me escape my daily mental anguish;
The verbal beatings I'd subject myself to
Because I felt like I deserved it.

Now, I realize how
Everything I went through,
Was for my highest good.
I perceive my time here as a blessing;
No longer resonating with feeling cursed and
defeated.
I was put here for a reason.

I've survived circumstances that I, once, thought were my final destination
Until I noticed I had the opportunities, resources, and tools to change it.
I have pushed forward through my struggles
With determination and resistance-
Shielding myself whenever it was needed.

I found myself after dealing with trials and tribulations.
Not even realizing how lost I was
Until I glanced back and saw myself from a distance;
Discovering that
I can't quite recognize that girl I once was.
Even though I know it's me-
There's no real familiarity.
I understand her,
But, I don't relate to the mindset she had
Because I've changed that.
The poetry I've written throughout my life
Can relay that.
Reinforcing that I have shifted from dark skies to a beautiful golden hue
I've survived hard times
And so can you.

Hollow Victories

Why don't I feel more proud of myself?
I won a poetry slam last night for my first time,
And it was the second time I ever performed in a poetry slam.
I tried to talk myself out of it yesterday morning-
But told myself I was being ridiculous and had nothing to lose.
I felt so fucking alive.
The crowd loved it.
I loved it.
But, now I feel kind of empty inside.
Is it that I can't feel proud of myself?
I DID feel proud, I even cried a little off and on,
But, it's like there's a hole within that makes me feel numb to pride.
It kind of felt like a hollow victory;
Even though, I know, it should mean quite a bit to me.
It simply doesn't hold that weight over me.
I want to go back,
And I do feel like my win was deserved-
But I couldn't help but think about the girl that I competed against-
Probably feeling defeated and upset.

I told her that her poem was great as we passed each other on the stairs and she just glanced down, mumbled thanks,
I kind of think she resented the fact that I was there.
If I wasn't, she would have won.
It's not my fault if I can perform better than others but why on earth does that make me feel selfish and like I should pass on opportunities to make someone else feel special?
What in this distorted mindfuck IS THIS?
Is it a problem with acceptance?
Or
Is it not a problem at all?
Maybe it's because I just don't need validation.
And I'm not here to win.
So maybe that's why I diminish it
Instead of celebrating.
I feel guilty for having this gift of mine sometimes and I can't quite understand why.
I denied it for so long
Because I didn't want to believe it.
Although, I knew because every person who reads my poems tells me
"You should write a book."
Well, I am.
It's about damn time, too.

Having Boundaries Is Self Care

Sometimes I get this inkling of a feeling
That something huge is waiting around the corner for me.
It's not, yet, accessible though.
I feel like I am going to have a massive breakthrough in love-
But, I do know, some obstacles and self-limiting beliefs must, first, be dealt with.
How many times have I rushed blindly into a situation-
To, discover later,
I have been robbed-
Physically and mentally?
Monetarily used? Verbally abused?
Failed relationships one after another,
One by one;
I'm the common denominator.
It doesn't mean I was bad to these people-
I've been a little too kind, too much of a push over, a people pleaser, too much of acting like I'm somebody's mother-
When really,
I needed MY mother.

I didn't want to believe her when she would warn me against trying to go after the love I so desperately desired.
She claimed I was being foolish;
Acting like a stubborn child.
I thought she wanted me to be alone and miserable-
What a fucking illusion...
Now, I see so clearly how she tried to protect me.
I didn't want to let her.
I pushed her out.
Because I didn't want to believe that she was right.
I had hope in these people.
And she saw right through their eyes-
Each and every one of them.
Something I can finally understand,
Because, unfortunately,
Sometimes, I have needed a wake up call
In order to snap me out of the spell of delusion.

Those epiphanies have been my savior
Granting me with newfound clarity;
There used to be an inability to properly
Understand exactly how
I was the problem in many of my interpersonal connections, until I did some deeper introspection.

I was the problem by not having boundaries-
And when I would set them;
These people would push me.
Yes, they were manipulative and took
advantage-
But my lack of self-control and self-care were
my disadvantage.

A Little Bit of Peace Was All I Needed

I realized somewhat recently that I've had body dysmorphia since I was a child.
I used to believe stupid things like having beauty marks made me ugly. Even though no one could see most of them.
Id cover my knees because I had this one beauty mark that was huge
Over time,
It's shrunk;
Just like my desire to give a fuck.
There's so many other things I should be worried about instead of what I look like.
I used to fear showing my body and face because I felt like a fat disgrace.
Now, I speak kindly to this body of mine that's overcome injuries, surgery, and has dealt with chronic pain over time.
When I speak nicely to myself,
The physicial pain isn't as bad
Probably because I'm not telling myself that's all I am.
I'm not some weak, sick, individual
Although, I damn sure have some medical issues.

I used to think what I told myself didn't matter
Because I thought *I* didn't matter.
When you switch that narrative around,
You'll see the blessings abound;
Filling in those negative spaces you set aside
And filling them with sunshine.

Do You Need To Fix Your Ship?

You are at the sail of your own ship.
If your mast is torn;
Ripped -
Improvise by using something you already have
to repair it.
You always have resources,
If you look a little further -
Beyond the veil of doubt.

We may break,
But we can rejuvenate ourselves
Picking up the pieces over the years.
Surrender your fears and rejoice in the
Freedom that entails when you release your
tears.
Whether they've built up,
Or just begun,
Each one sheds a past version of yourself-
Allowing you to heal from grief, heartache,
betrayal, and, overall sorrow-
Inviting opportunities to go towards
The simple pleasures and joy that life can bring;
But, first, we must release the pain,
So we can embrace tomorrow in a new way
And the happiness we are able to attain.

I Am The Epitome of Creativity

Attune to the frequency
The higher vibrations that lead you to me,
And, I to thee.
Following your dreams
As I follow mine,
Keep the hope and positivity alive-
Because that's how you allow yourself to properly shine.
Creativity brings me prosperity.
Nothing gives me more energy than
Creating something that hits me on a different level;
That perfect synergy.
It fills me with appreciation
That I was able to create a great piece
And gratitude that I am finally allowing my words to flow free.

These words flow through me;
Like an overflowing sink.
Escaping as quickly as they've accumulated
Running onto the floor
Flooding me out with their power.
I'm drowning in poetic fiber.

So enriching for the soul.
For mine.
For yours.
It's fodder for my mouth to chew on,
Spitting out the little bits that don't make much sense.
Letting the words take control and
Indulging in the way these poems light up my insides; the fire within my core.
Allowing the messages that are seeping through my pores to excrete what my mind speaks.
My hands feel like they're burning with
Electricity,
As I write down the words that flow to me.
Bouncing around in my brain until they make it on to a page.
I am the epitome of creativity.

Robbed By Procrastination

Procrastination pulls me apart
Limb by limb.
Why do I do it?
I figured I had more time
Then, it seems the "time" I thought I had escapes me...
And my anxiety runs in,
Because, now, I'm late once again.
Delayed responsibilities
Returning to be completed,
While I ignore them and entertain
Things that don't really give me any gain.
Like taking an extra cigarette break and getting lost in the ribbons of exhaled smoke;
They look so beautiful-
Yet, cause me to choke.
Sometimes the things we love eventually kill us.
I wish I didn't love smoking.
And, sometimes, I don't.
I recognize how it's robbed me of opportunities and leaves me in financial constraints
Ones that I have chosen
Because I have the choice to quit
Although, I never feel like I'm actually ready yet.

Will I be ready when it causes physical distress?
Or will I keep smoking because of my stress?
When is enough, enough?
Will it be when cancer creeps in,
Knocks on my window
While I'm asleep in bed?
Or will I keep smoking, even then?

Don't Waste Your Water on Plants That Refuse To Grow

I feel it flowing through my veins;
I am abundance.
And, in abundance, I shall remain.

Forever protected and on the right path that lead
me to the divine.
The light they shine
Doesn't blind me anymore,
Because I know they're surrounding me
With supportive energy.
Comforting me when I feel anxiety,
And encouraging me to pursue my aspirations
and dreams.
They escort me
To the destinations
That will fulfill me.
The places that fill me with energy;
Immersing me in baths filled with spirituality.

My relationship with them has evolved and
transformed my views on life and who I am.
They have shown me who I am-
As if it were third person,
And I was watching myself.

They showed me how genuinely good hearted I am,
After dealing with fraudulent counterparts who were downright crooked and bad.
Only out for themselves,
Because they don't give a fuck about anyone else.
I've been lied to, cheated on, stabbed in the back,
While remaining consistent,
Trying to build these people up-
But, they were too busy being sad and pathetic to notice or give a fuck.

I have witnessed those whom have wronged me
Go through heavy karmic events
Soon after I ditched their ass.
I couldn't help but chuckle;
Because the karma you reap when you fuck with someone pure hearted and loyal,
Is double the amount of soil-
Burying the seed you tried to plant and
Suffocating it's plans.
The evil some people have put me through,
I've witnessed return tenfold to them.
One ex, in particular, every time we argued about something he picked a fight with me on,
He would get hurt in some shape or form.
The realization, after a while,

Was that I wasn't in the wrong and karma was hitting him where it hurt because I was a good soul he was putting through hell.

Years later, I know, I definitely was not in the wrong.
He is a covert narcissist.
Blamed me for his hardships when he couldn't see it was really him.
I was kind, I helped pay his bills, got him a phone, a new bed because his old one had coils bulging out of the mattress, helped him finish school, tried to encourage him to pursue a career he loved, stocked his shelves with groceries,
Because his parents were strung out on heroin and couldn't afford meals, I did his laundry, cleaned up after him, and the list goes on.
I recognize now,
I treated him like he was a son;
And, I, the motherly nurturer.
But, you can't nurture
What is rotten and refuses to grow.
You can pour water on the soil
But if they refuse to absorb it,
You're just wasting water on a plant
That wishes it was already dead.
So it declines to drink
So it can die a quicker death;
Bitter resent that you even attempted to water it.
Because they didn't ask for it.

Now, I Know Myself

None of us asked to be here-
On this earth.
For what it's worth,
You've gotta make the most of the blessings that life gives,
Itself.
I'm grateful I was put here.
A Planted seed that eventually grew into a tree
Now here to spread my roots
I tried so hard to die
Overdose after overdose because I felt cursed, stressed, and depressed.
I couldn't see my purpose
I couldn't see the uplifting energy I brought because I felt shut out.
That old version of me severed such a higher purpose than I ever could have previously seen.
Before reality shifted for me,
My old mindsets began to die off,
Ego deaths. Shedding false facets of what I previously determined to be the truth
Because, sometimes, illusions can distort you.

Erasure of mental distress-
All because I found myself,

After experiencing severe failed conquests to achieve death, wake up calls, tests I passed without even knowing but passed without much effort because I paid attention to the lessons presented.
How would I know that staying a little longer in certain places would lead me to success?
Those circumstances brought me more gratitude and appreciation than I'll ever be able to express or decree so I'll just say it over and over again because it's motivational to me!

I'm grateful.
Grateful to be alive.
Grateful for the wisdom life provides.
Grateful I am able to know how to use and trust my discernment.
Grateful the universe saved me from suicides I tried to commit when I felt like I should have deserved it.
Grateful I was able to forgive myself for the darkness that I felt.
Grateful I was able to shift my life,
And get out.

Out of the depressed mindset, of the toxic relationships, of the need for someone else to be my everything,
Because I learned I'm all I ever needed.

It wasn't until after my attempts and some karmic relationships that I learned more about myself.
I dug deeper
Because I was only able to see the surface-
Until others began to point things out to me that made more sense;
About what I was doing to myself and others,
And why I felt like any of us deserved it or like I was a burden to everyone and their mother.
I started healing my own wounds,
Daily cleansing, protective auras, evil eye wards, and crystals galore.
But, it's spirituality itself that has always charmed and adored.

It brought me closer to myself,
And helped me work on the things that needed to be mended in order for my life to take a different spin than the typical cycles it was used to being in.
Now, I have a better appreciation for this life-
The one I once used to hate
Until I learned how to embrace.
Knowing that boundless inspiration
Comes from the pain I've had to face.

Life Gets Better If You Just Hold On

Oh, how lost I was-
Back then.
Looking back on my past reveals darkness I withheld.
And knowing who I am now, illuminates
The shadows
Of my former self.
Shining down on the things I didn't use to understand-
It took me tremendous willpower and strength to pull myself out of my delusional hell.
I went from assuming I was cursed since the day of my birth,
To gaining wisdom on how I have a purpose
And just what that is.
Part of that, is this.
Sharing my life stories,
My journey,
How I went from a mindset of doom and gloom and transmuted it into the life I always dreamed of having;
The one I longed for-
But, I wasn't attempting because I had too much anxiety.

Too much fear.

It used to feel as if I wasn't actually living;
As if I were some sort of dead girl walking.
And, I wasn't living.
I was idling;
Letting time pass on by.
Going down the wrong roads,
Until I got stopped
By forces of the unknown,
Who steered me the right way,
Little by little,
Until one day, I found myself standing in front of a microphone.
I think I should feel disbelief
But, I don't because I've closed out cycles of my past
That left me incomplete.
And followed the way my heart led me.
And that was to poetry.
My parents were encouraging
But, previously, I couldn't see my worth and thought my life was ugly.
That's the beauty of it-
The pain I allow myself to bare
Shows confidence while pursuing the passions that provide me with bliss.
I am grateful my body didn't quit
When I tried to give in

Because I wouldn't have discovered how good
Life truly is.

Discover Yourself

Break down your walls
And answer the calls
To your inner truths.
Allow guidance to assist you,
Whenever it's needed.
If you feel like there's nobody there;
Whisper to spirit;
Because it does care.
You may not feel it-
But by speaking,
You're releasing
What no longer serves you and is causing despair,
Rather than dwelling in sorrow's care.
If you know what you want in life-
Don't give in to those passive doubts that it won't work out.
Get out there and achieve it,
So you can prove it to yourself!

If you can't figure out your purpose,
You better go within yourself
Before you begin to succumb to thoughts of feeling worthless; aimless.

Searching each direction looking for a quick fix
to your solutions and feeling frustrated and
impatient.
That will only keep you feeling misguided and
anxious.

Get up inside your mind and discover where
your true passion lies beyond any doubts that
may bind you and keep you trapped inside.
What makes you thrive and feel energized?
Like a fire burning you up inside?
What encourages your drive?
Making you motivated to start your day the
moment you wake because you're excited about
the path you decided to take?

If you stop allowing external influences
To counteract your dreams and visions,
And listen to your intuition,
You will recognize that you know yourself better
than anyone else.
You're not their perception.
Be aware when spirit is talking to you-
The inner knowledge, with which, it provides Is
there for you to accept it.

Embrace: What fills you with life, excitement,
and feeling like your life is being aligned;

Things that enlighten and give you the fuel for your journey's ride.

And

Release: What devoids you of hope, joy, inspiration, and personal contentment;
Those are disruptive to your senses and keep you stuck and misdirected.

Pay attention to the signs;
Your body knows when it feels right and when it doesn't-
It's your internal compass that tells you the correct path;
Your body and mind will tell you "This isn't the right way. You have to stop doing this."

If you pay attention,
You'll walk down the correct roads
Some with blessings, others with lessons, and always with the opportunity to learn and grow.
Eventually, you'll find the road to completing
Your personal life purpose and mission
Purely by listening to and accepting your intuition.

As humans, we have free will and can choose to embark down the wrong path;

Although that one teaches lessons that you can, later, transmute into advice for the masses if they choose to listen.
You can talk about prevention and possibly help someone naive to the situation.
Your entire journey has more meaning than you may be able to recognize now.
But have faith and push forward with determination and recognize the importance of the wisdom you've been given.

Speaking Some Of My Truths

I perform yoga,
Non-traditionally;
In the form of poetry
By writing and releasing my pain.
I bend the words that line each page
To fit the channeled messages I'm trying to relay.
Putting them on display for the audience to
interpret and reflect on in each of their own
ways.
I have lived in heaven,
And,
I have lived in hell.
The stories of my life
Compelled to be dug up and released-
So I can have inner peace
Knowing there's someone out there who needs to
hear me speak.
If I don't speak up and out
About injustices I, and others have been dealt
I'm an accomplice to madness;
Unrighteousness for all because I kept it to
myself.
That's just selfish.
I refuse to be a sheep,

Because I'm the wolf-
Hunting down the truth and exposing the false.

I have been naive
Which has shown me more than enough about the motives of others.
And the actions I've done myself.
Many times I have felt like I had a mirror held up before me;
So I could take a deeper look at what I was allowing
To happen with my health
Physically and mentally
Because when you're surrounded by dark;
You eventually start to lose yourself..
I didn't always know how to love myself
because I was, once, surrounded by overt and covert narcissists
And each one had me in their clutch.
It always felt like the problem was me until I found a relationship that brought me
clarity.

We barely argued, he didn't make me feel crazy, he was supportive and the perfect energy for me to understand it really wasn't me.
Because I could vibe with him synergistically.
That relationship ended and I found myself with another narcissist-

This one; a sociopath who couldn't keep his lies in check.
He made me out to be a problem while I was supporting both of us the entire time,
And I was recovering from a fusion surgery on my right foot while he robbed me blind.
He played with my sanity, made me out to be the enemy.
When, really, it was him projecting.

I realized, by then,
What he was saying were mere lies.
I knew I wasn't a bad girlfriend because of everything I had done for him time after time.
I got myself into a mess but didn't know if I could climb out of it.
I'm grateful that I did.

Using my previous relationship as a comparison,
I recalled how we hardly ever argued, let alone shouted.
Any disagreements were discussed like adults.
Not shouting at me that I'm a "stupid fucking cunt".
I sat there while he screamed at me over tiny things that weren't worth me showing emotions or arguing over,

Then, him calling me an unemotional bitch because I don't respond to adults who act like toddlers.
The week prior to that argument, he said I'm "too emotional",
AS IF..
So I chuckled while he called me names and flipped his shit.
Desperate to get a reaction out of me and laughter wasn't supposed to be it
But, he was just over the top ridiculous.
I am grateful I learned how to be grounded before meeting him
And got on medication for my new journey; my discovery that I have adhd.

I attempted suicide twice the year prior, in 2020 before meeting the devil presenting himself as someone worthy of my heart's desires.
He was the opposite of everything he claimed to be.
Opposite of everything that I stand for and believe,
But, he matched my answers to questions to lure me.
He was racist, selfish, egotistical, an anti feminist, viewed himself as the savior when he, instead, torments others, acted like a dictator, a know-it-all who didn't know jack but believed

himself so much that he didn't think I'd inquire or look things up and call him out once I figured the truth out.

He catfishes his friends and puts them through unnecessary aggravation and stress.
Pretends to be anybody and everybody except himself,
Because he never allowed himself to go within and find the people who matched his vibe.

He just goes from one relationship to the next to see how much he can get out of each one;
Leaving them drained and late on rent because he took money from them and now, their savings have been spent.

They call a man who goes from one relationship to the next a hobosexual and God only knows where that dude has been because they'll live on anyone's couch and use sex to pay rent.

Stay away from people who try to rush and pressure you;
And, know, you're a treasure
That has to wait to be touched
By the right kind of person.
Not by someone who seems down on their luck but, really, they're a leech who sucks the life out

of you, leaves you in debt, and in need of a
series of counseling sessions to discuss all the
fucked up turns of events.

If you do find yourself in a shady situation-
person or place,
Know it's an opportunity to learn lessons
That, one day, can be displayed in a way that
helps you and others get through the rain;
Like performing it as poetry on a stage.

Art is the most beautiful way to express the
emotions you encounter, especially your pain.
The words you speak might save someone or
make them reflect on their own experiences and
feelings.
Causing them to question belief systems that
were previously limited.
You'd be surprised at what inspires others to get
on with their life and leave what's in their past
behind.
Words are empowering-
But, the actions motivated by affirmations and
encouragement
Are my favorite kind.

Ghastly Gaslighting

If I were a ghost,
I think I'd like to mess with the heads of several, select exes.
Gaslight them the way they did to me.
Make them question their sanity.
Whisper into the ears of their loved ones about how they're truly fucking crazy.
Ideas of a poltergeist fantasy
How I can turn the TV off while they're involved in a video game;
Turn the water ice cold when they take a shower,
Set the toast setting to high so theirs will burn,
Put some sharp objects in their bedsheets...
It's only fair since they're a fucking prick, too.
This all sounds a little savage,
But compared to what they put me through,
It's not even remotely close to balanced.
It would only be for me to laugh a little at their pain.
I could write on the walls of the apartment where they live alone,
Randomly knock over objects
Like I'm a non-existent cat,
Shut their dryer off while their clothes are still damp,

Mix up their cleaning products so they're all in different bottles.
Good luck figuring out which one is which tomorrow!
Considering I'd be invisible, I'd wait until the middle of the night to ruin their rugs and furniture.
I could exchange the multi-purpose cleaner for bleach,
And watch as they struggle to clean it up,
Trying to figure out which product is which, and how the products got switched?!
But, although I'd love to fuck with them,
I don't think I'd be able to commit-
Because I don't have the same darkness in my head;
Contrary to everything I just said because that took me a while to come up with!
8 minutes to come up with some quick wit.
Normally, I can pump out a poem in 5 minutes, but this one took me 10.
Double the imagination,
Double the time,
Double the amount of validation that
I am not of their kind.

Unconventional Poet

I'm an unconventional poet;
Taking snippets of my life's wisdom
And bearing my soul;
I expose-
The light and the dark.
Words I compose
On line embedded paper
Or on my phone.
I enjoy straying from the norm
Because I am not of the typical form.

I concluded long ago,
That I am a black sheep.
I used to try to fit in-
But, there wasn't any space for me,
So I strayed from the crowd
And now I'm here reading my poetry aloud.

I've been writing since I was a child
I found that poetry fueled me with intense
desire; inspired.
The words that are spoken
By the ones who, once, felt voiceless,
Are my favorite to mentally acquire.
Creativity is passion,

Passion is to have an affinity.
Affinity, for me,
IS passion and creativity.
Right here, I look around the lounge,
And I see a community.
We are the voices of diversity,
Allowing others in to bear witness to our stories.
There is strength in unity.
And right here, is infinite opportunity.

Power behind our words because they're
stemming from life's curves and what we've
learned.
You don't have to rhyme to be a poet!
You just have to sit down and allow yourself to
live in the moment.
Whatever flows from your wrists to your
fingertips,
Is considered a piece of art that was created from
your heart.
And I find that, the most beautiful part.

Life Shoved Me In The Right Direction

Life has a funny way or redirecting you when you're going the wrong way.
I love my job.
I'm a pet sitter.
But I've had issue after issue,
Physical ailments, neurotic clients I had to abandon,
Some crazy cats and dogs
And a few that were sweet and didn't cause destruction or harm.
I have repeating roadblocks
And I walk around or climb over the obstacles
And...
Life grows annoyed,
Because it's trying to teach me without me getting hurt,
But, most Taureans are stubborn anyway.
We are the bull.
So I charge each obstacle,
And with every shove through, I become more wounded
Yet, still,
Somehow stronger in the end.

I can see what life is doing.
Clearly this isn't meant for me.
You know what is?
Poetry.
Spoken words that have slept within an urn.
They're ready to rise from the dead and
Commence a comeback that has, long been,
Deserved.

A Little Grief

Memories of the past seem to fade
When the people I love pass away.
Sometimes, almost as if they were never even here...
But, traces of them are left behind;
Not only in the belongings they've left;
But, also, in the remaining visions I still preserve in my mind.
Grief is a strange process and never quite linear.
We all heal at our own pace-
Some give up or attempt suicide
Because they can't bear the pain.
I understand that feeling so well because
Fear used to flow through my veins.
Many times, I was stuck in my own hell
Refusing to look at the bright side,
Because I was bitter and enraged.
The only suffrage that was created was my own.
I've always told myself to put my pain in words.
So...
I did release some heartache in the midst of my grief-
Although, I wasn't quite mentally present
Enough to properly participate.
This resulted in a lot of unfinished work-

Too many scattered one or two line attempts at poems
That I've procrastinated sifting through,
Since there's too many directions they've been cast into.
It's overwhelming,
But, little by little,
I may be able to build a story
Purely by incorporating every unfinished note stored away in my phone.
They thought I had abandoned them,
But one day, all those, once meaningless, scrambled thoughts and feelings
Will find their way into a book.
One that I can hold,
Knowing I gave meaning back
To the words that haven't been told.

Bass Soothes My Soul

There's something about bass that soothes me.
The pumps to my chest-
I feel it in my heart with each beat.
The rush it creates,
Makes my mind retreat,
And enjoy the moment.
Embracing the punches to my heart,
After all, it's a feeling I know best.
I become entranced and can't help but dance,
My lips matching every word because I'm actually singing aloud.
The music drowning me out because it's too loud.

Memorizing lyrics to heal my sickness.
Daily affirmation messages,
Helping me understand certain lessons,
So I can shift through cycles with quickness.
With ease.
Peaceful promises of new beginnings through random passages and synchronicities sent to me.
Signs from the divine
That I'm walking the right line
Witnessing my life align
Before my shiny eyes.

Music, poetry, art, and creativity
Are so inspiring;
Rewarding to the open mind
As you consume the words you listen to
Throughout time.
Evolving one layer after another,
When you fill yourself with with genuine positive intent,
To correct any negative dialect you have been fed.
I chose to listen to more upbeat music to see if it would affect my mindset.
And it did.
Make sure you fill your mental tank with things that bring you peace and content,
So you can focus
On the joy you understand best.

Live Out Your Dreams

Live out your dreams;
Things don't have to be as dark as they may seem.
Don't ignore the truth of reality,
And the opportunities you will meet.
Along the way,
The feelings of doubt will retreat.
If you look beyond the horizon,
You'll see there's more reasons to live than reasons to die.

Don't hide your light; shine it
Because others need to find it.
When you feel broken and defeated,
Remember that you're simply going through a stormy season.
You have perseverance;
Have faith that better days will come
No storm lasts forever.
Eventually, the clouds dissipate,
The sky illustrates rainbows
After the rain.
Proving that beauty can arise from dark, gloomy days.
The way you perceive life

Can make it feel great,
Or -- Laced with sorrow, anger, and pain.

Don't let the dark thoughts bind and blindside you
You worked so hard to get this far.
So don't give in, don't give up.
Keep up the fight and hold on when you're on a bumpy ride
Make the most of the time that we have left in this life.
Don't waste it away-
Thinking you are, already, rotted and decayed.

"So, what's the point anyway?"
You're worth so much more than what you think you deserve.

What you give to others will, indeed, be returned.
Make sure you're spreading love while you remain on this earth.
Even to those who you think don't deserve.
Give, but don't over extend-
And, be sure to protect yourself from sinister intent.

You're more than a body, more than the color of your skin, and so much more than if you're fat or you're thin;
You are consciousness within.
You are a beautiful soul underneath what resides on the surface.
Adjust your mirror if you can't see too clearly,
So you'll be able to see the true, genuine beauty.
Its not your external reflection;
It's the person beneath the flesh and bones;
It's the soul inside of you that brilliantly glows.

www.ingramcontent.com/pod-product-compliance
Lightning Source LLC
Chambersburg PA
CBHW051736130826
49812CB00033B/888
9789357440592